SCHOOL FUN

PUZZLES • MAZES • WORD GAMES

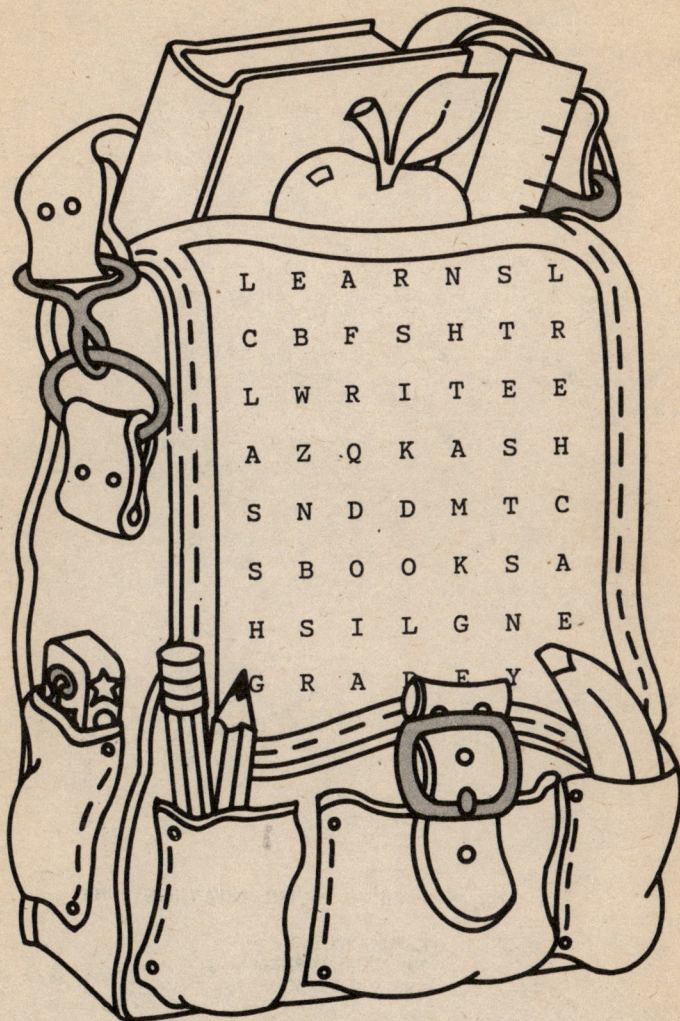

```
L E A R N S L
C B F S H T R
L W R I T E E
A Z Q K A S H
S N D D M T C
S B O O K S A
H S I L G N E
G R A D E Y
```

kidsbooks
Incorporated

Hurry! It's time to get to school!
Travel through this maze by following the letters
that correctly spell...

SCHOOL DAYS

3

In the puzzle below, find and circle all
these words relating to school.

BOOKS   MATH
CLASS   READ
ENGLISH   TEACHER
GRADE   TEST
LEARN   WRITE

```
L E A R N S L
C B F S H T R
L W R I T E E
A Z Q K A S H
S N D D M T C
S B O O K S A
H S I L G N E
G R A D E Y T
```

4

SEE ANSWER SECTION

How many things can you find wrong in this picture? Circle them.

A APPLE   B CAR   C CAT   D DOG

$$+\frac{2}{\cancel{2}}{5} \quad +\frac{3}{6}{9} \quad +\frac{5}{1}{7}$$

SEE ANSWER SECTION

Which two pencils are exactly the same?
Circle them.

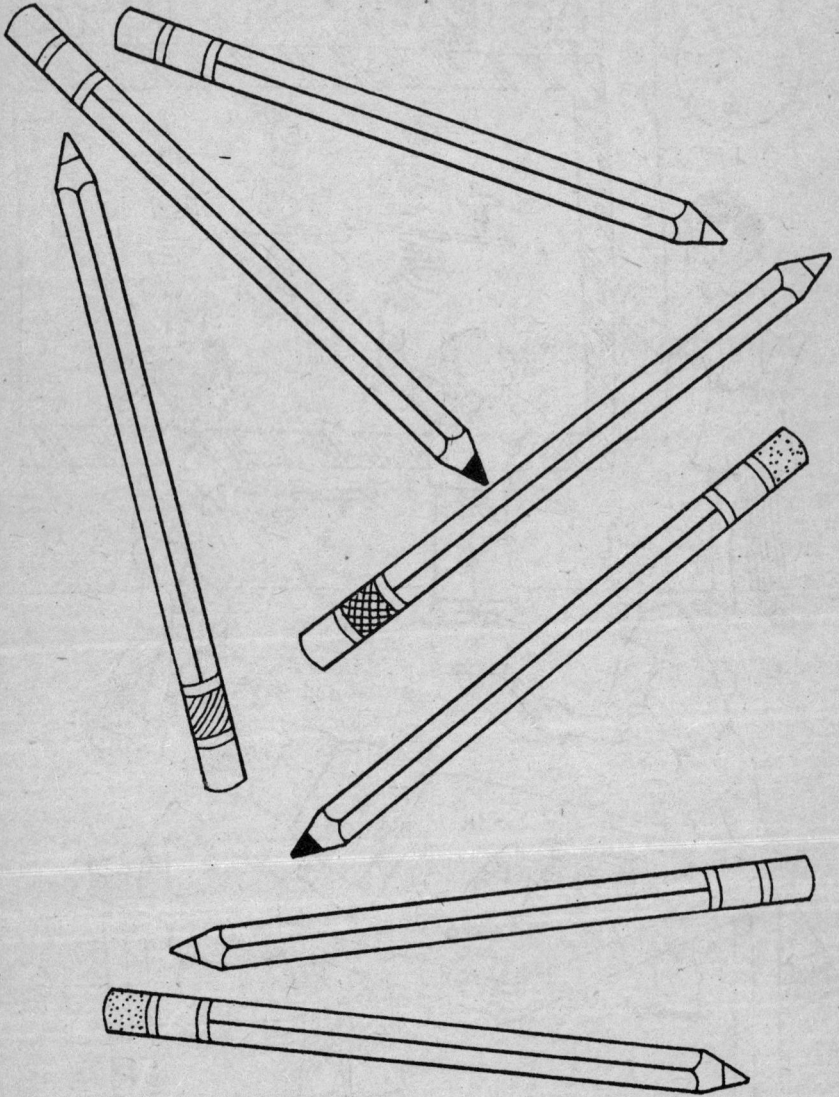

6

Answer each clue. Then place the circled letters
in their correct places below to complete
the mystery sentence.

OPPOSITE OF UP. (D)own
$\overline{6}$ _ _ _

3 PLUS 1 EQUALS ____ . (F)our
$\overline{1}$ _ _ _

THE MONTH AFTER MAY. _ _ O _
$\overline{5}$

NOT SMALL. _ O _
$\overline{3}$

YOU HEAR WITH THESE. O _ O _
$\overline{4}$ $\overline{2}$

YOUR TEACHER IS YOUR $\overline{1}$ $\overline{2}$ $\overline{3}$ $\overline{4}$ $\overline{5}$ $\overline{6}$.

SEE ANSWER SECTION

What does everyone look forward to around the middle of a school day? To find out, cross out all the **A, G, P,** and **S** letters in the puzzle. Then, list the remaining letters, as they appear, in the blank spaces below.

L	A	U	P
S	N	C	G
H	G	A	T
A	I	P	S
M	S	G	E

__ __ __ __ __   __ __ __ __ !

SEE ANSWER SECTION

Everyone brought an apple for the teacher! Which two are exactly alike? Circle them.

9

Who helps run your school? Fill in the
areas that have a dot • to find out.

Travel through this maze by correctly
spelling the word—

C L A S S R O O M .

Write these words in their correct spaces.

3 letters
PEN

6 letters
LESSON

5 letters
ERASE
NOTES
PAPER
STUDY
THINK

SEE ANSWER SECTION

How many times does the word **PENCIL** appear in this puzzle? Circle each one.

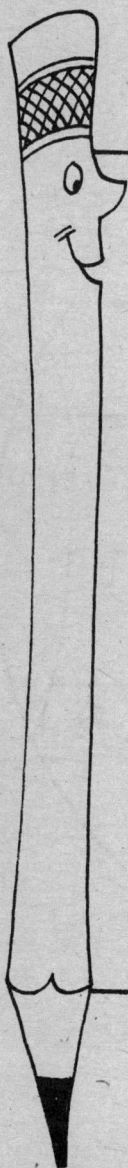

```
L   I   C   N   E   P

B   F   K   M   L   L

P   E   N   C   I   L

C   J   O   C   C   I

D   P   N   S   N   C

G   E   T   V   E   N

P   H   W   A   P   E

Q   R   O   Z   B   P
```

TOTAL: _____

SEE ANSWER SECTION

Where can you still play basketball when it's raining outside? Cross out the letters in the boxes that have a square □. Then write the remaining letters, as they appear, in the spaces below.

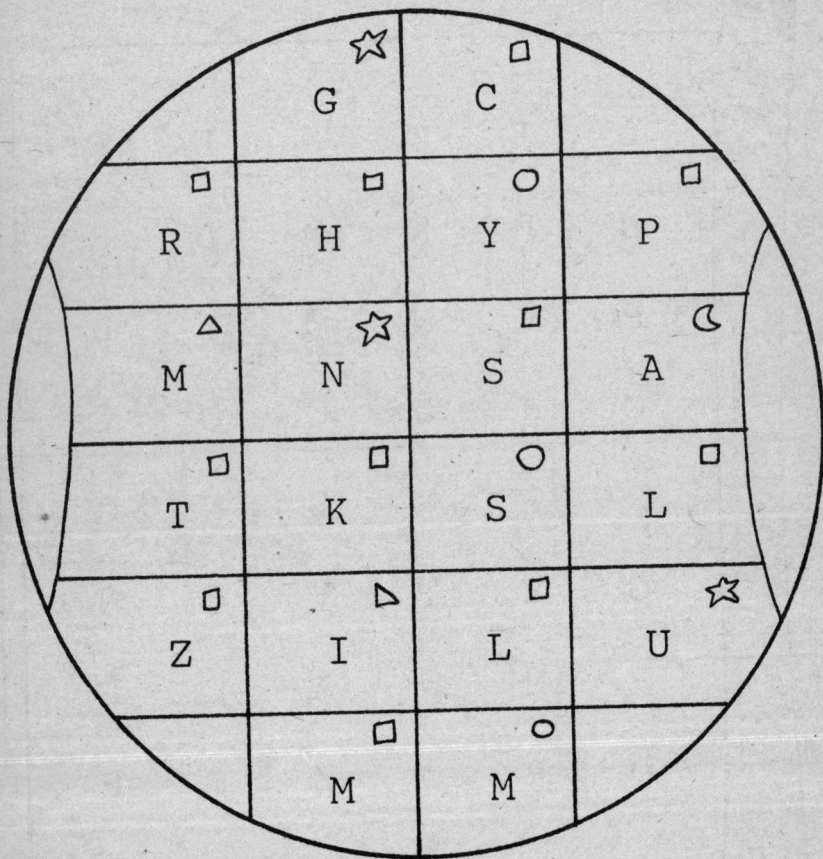

THE _ _ _ _ _ _ _ _ _ !

SEE ANSWER SECTION

Can you solve this crossword puzzle?

across

3. George Washington was our country's first _____.
5. What you eat in the cafeteria.

down

1. A red fruit.
2. You write with this.
4. Six plus four equals ___.

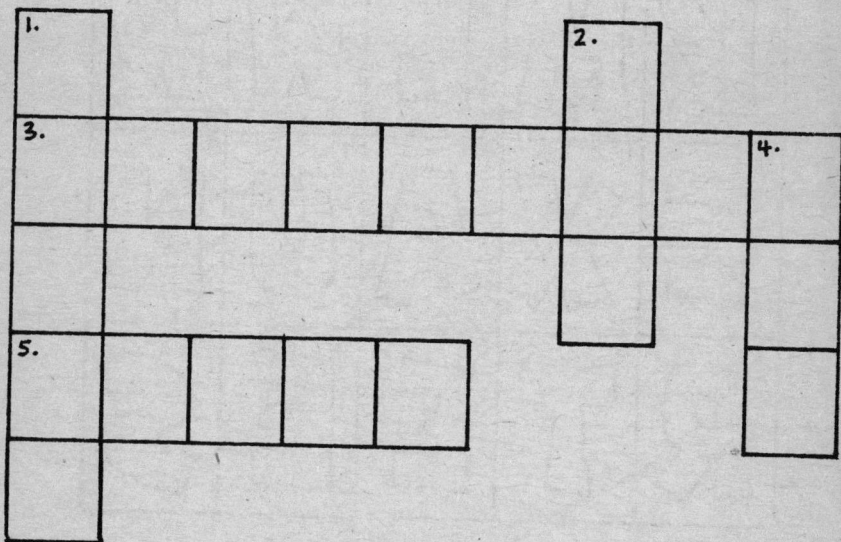

Cross out all the even numbered letters. Then write the remaining letters, as they appear, in the spaces below.

¹⁰ Y	⁵ C	⁴ R	³ L	⁸ Z
¹ A	² T	⁷ S	⁵ S	⁶ I
⁴ K	⁹ M	⁸ L	¹² W	² W
⁸ E	⁶ X	¹ A	⁴ U	⁶ N
² R	⁵ T	³ E	¹⁰ E	⁷ S

_ _ _ _ _ _ _ _ _ _

SEE ANSWER SECTION

Where is a good place to go when you want to read or study? Travel through this maze to reach the answer.

GO

THE LIBRARY

THE PLAYGROUND

THE GYMNASIUM

SEE ANSWER SECTION

In the puzzle below, find and circle these words that are used to describe teachers.

CARING   HELPFUL
CLEVER   KIND
COOL   PATIENT
FINE   SMART
FUNNY   WISE

```
C  L  E  V  E  R  T
A  U  E  L  O  O  C
R  F  K  W  F  A  C
I  P  I  I  U  D  S
N  L  N  S  N  H  M
G  E  D  E  N  R  A
L  H  H  C  Y  S  R
P  A  T  I  E  N  T
```

SEE ANSWER SECTION

How many things can you find wrong in this picture? Circle them.

Which backpack is different from the others? Find and circle it.

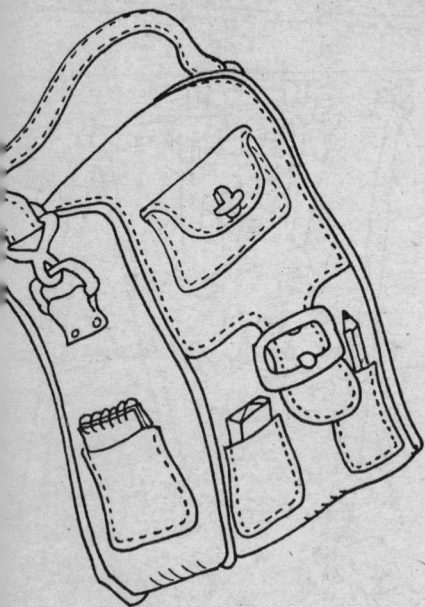

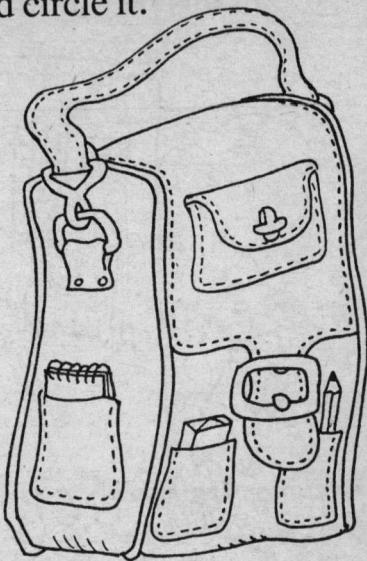

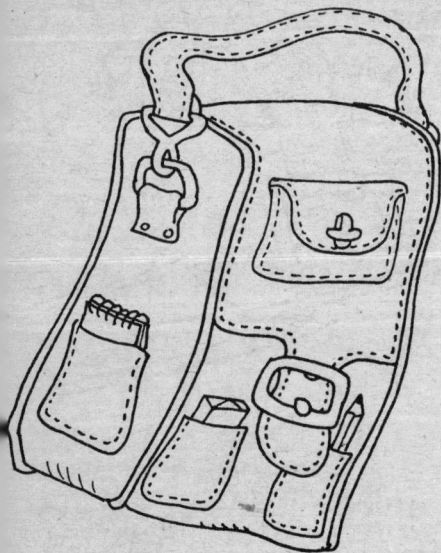

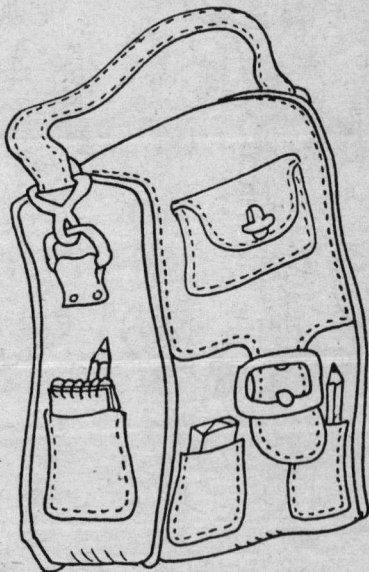

Unscramble these words having to do with school.

O B K O   — — — —

R D E A   — — — —

S L A C S   — — — — —

U B S   — — —

Y L A P   — — — —

N R A E L   — — — — —

SEE ANSWER SECTION

What can you always expect teachers to give to students? Cross out every **THIRD LETTER** and list the remaining letters, as they appear, in the spaces below.

	H		O	
T		M		E
	P		W	
O		F		R
	K		A	

— — — — — — — — — —

SEE ANSWER SECTION

How many textbooks do you see? (Count carefully, for many of them overlap.)

TOTAL: _____

SEE ANSWER SECTION

To reveal the hidden word, fill in the
areas that have a dot •

SEE ANSWER SECTION

Travel through this maze by correctly spelling the word—

A R I T H M E T I C .

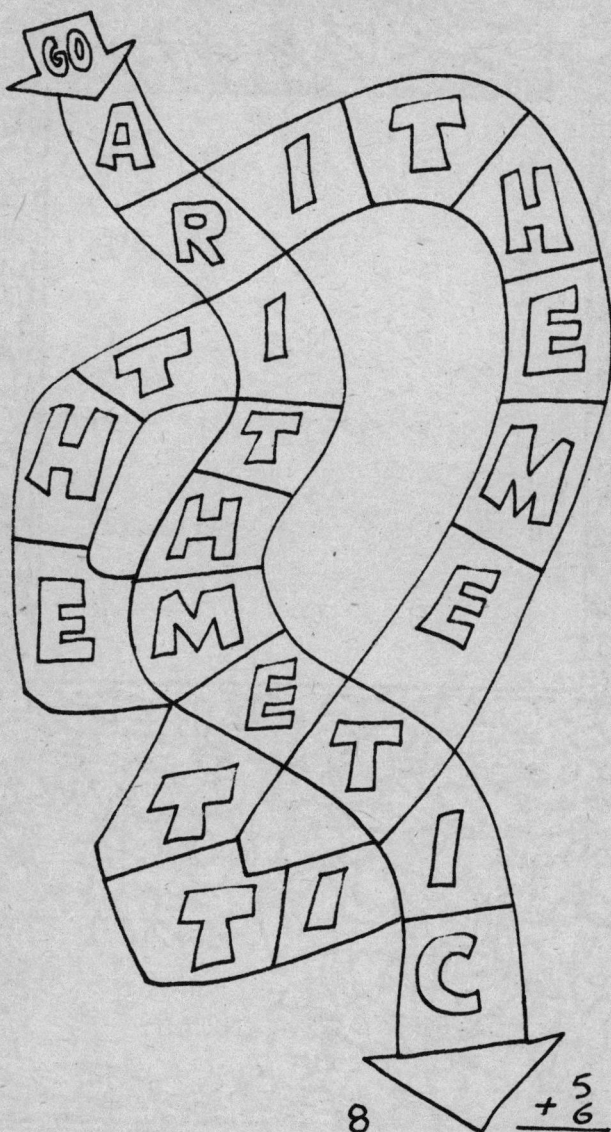

$$\begin{array}{r} 8 \\ + 9 \\ \hline 17 \end{array} \qquad \begin{array}{r} 5 \\ + 6 \\ \hline 11 \end{array}$$

SEE ANSWER SECTION

How many times does the word **BOOK** appear
in this puzzle? Circle each one.

D	B	O	O	K
B	J	G	L	B
O	R	N	K	O
O	F	O	H	O
K	O	O	B	K
B	B	O	O	K

TOTAL: _____

SEE ANSWER SECTION

Cross out all the letters in the boxes that have a star ✪. Write the remaining letters, as they appear, in the spaces below to complete the sentence.

S	T	B	U
U	D	M	D
Z	C	E	N
N	R	M	T
L	S	S	G

BE KIND TO YOUR FELLOW

_ _ _ _ _ _ _ _ !

Hidden in this picture
are all the numbers from **1** to **10**.
Find and circle them.

SEE ANSWER SECTION

Can you find the following hidden objects in this picture?

FISH   NECKTIE   TRIANGLE   FLOWER

BANANA   WRISTWATCH   KEY   PAINTBRUSH

Let's take a look at the teacher's desk.
Circle all the things that begin
with the letter "B."

30

SEE ANSWER SECTION

Which one of the children will reach the school bus? Follow each path and find out!

To find out what's fun, decode this
message by placing the letters in
the numbered spaces below.

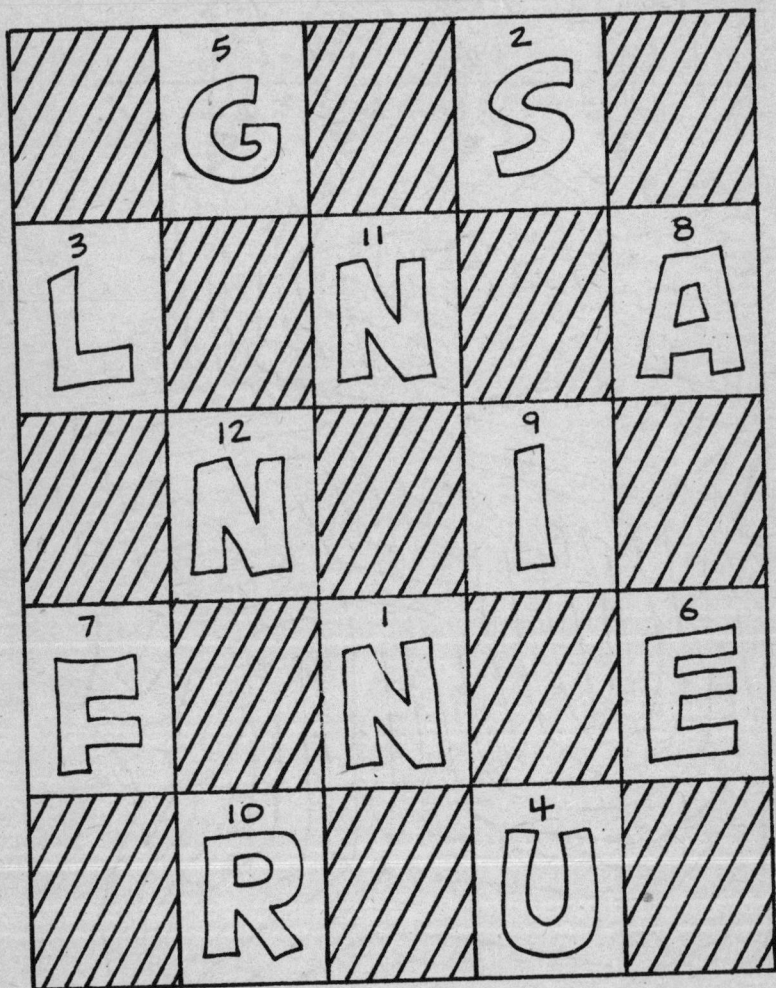

	G (5)		S (2)	
L (3)		Ñ (11)		A (8)
	N (12)		I (9)	
F (7)		N (1)		E (6)
	R (10)		U (4)	

$\overline{3}\ \overline{6}\ \overline{8}\ \overline{10}\ \overline{1}\ \overline{9}\ \overline{11}\ \overline{5}\qquad \overline{9}\ \overline{2}$

$\overline{7}\ \overline{4}\ \overline{12}$!

SEE ANSWER SECTION

Write the opposite of each word. Then place the circled letters in their correct spaces below to reveal the mystery word.

D A Y ⚪ _ _ _ ⚪
6 2

H A P P Y ⚪ _ ⚪
8 4

N O R T H ⚪ _ ⚪ _ _
1 3

F A L S E ⚪ _ _ _ ⚪
7 5

$\overline{1}$ $\overline{2}$ $\overline{3}$ $\overline{4}$ $\overline{5}$ $\overline{6}$ $\overline{7}$ $\overline{8}$

SEE ANSWER SECTION

What's YOUR favorite subject? To find the subject that is hidden in this puzzle, cross out all the **A, E, M,** and **W** letters in the chart. Then list the remaining letters, as they appear, in the blank spaces below.

H	M	I	A
W	E	S	M
A	T	W	O
W	E	R	W
Y	M	A	E

__ __ __ __ __ __ __

SEE ANSWER SECTION

34

Find and circle the following letters hidden in this picture.

A   B   C   D   E   F   G   H   I   J

Circle all the letters in the boxes that have a square ☐. Then write them, as they appear, in the spaces below to complete the sentence.

△ T	☐ F	☐ R	☽ Y
☐ I	☆ C	△ Q	○ K
☆ R	▽ F	○ S	☐ E
▷ Z	☐ N	△ G	○ L
☐ D	☽ R	☆ A	☐ S

SCHOOL IS A GREAT PLACE TO MAKE

NEW _ _ _ _ _ _ _ _ !

SEE ANSWER SECTION

Let's go out to the playground!
Circle all the things that start with the letter "S."

Can you write these playground words in their correct spaces?

<u>3 letters</u>
RUN
TAG

<u>5 letters</u>
GAMES
GRASS
LAUGH
THROW

SEE ANSWER SECTION

How many globes do you see?
Count carefully for many
of them overlap.

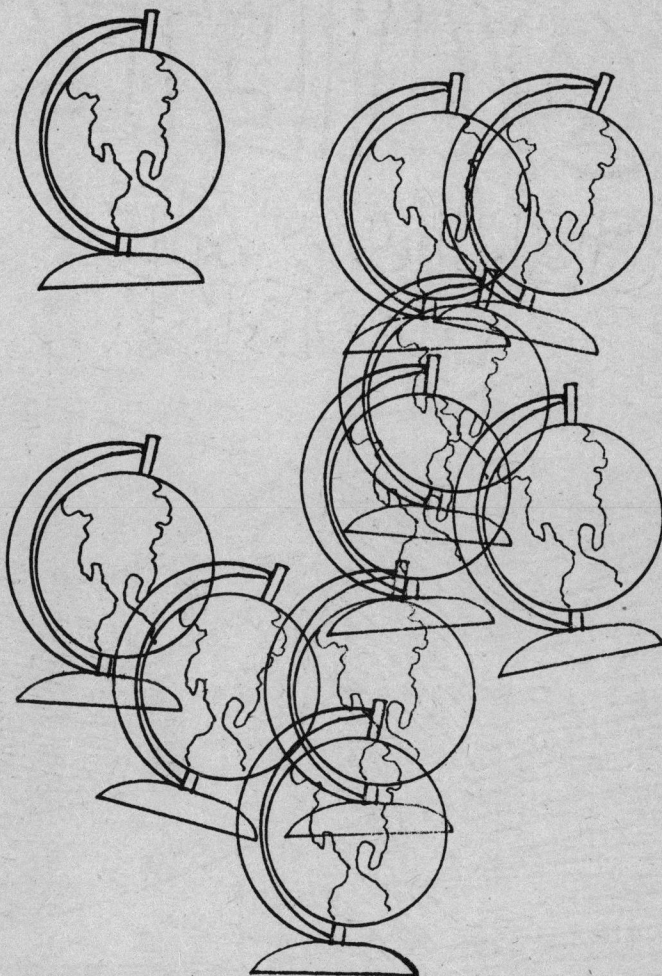

TOTAL: _____

Color, cut-out and display this
mini-poster.

QUIET!
GENIUS AT WORK!

A+

Go through this pencil maze.

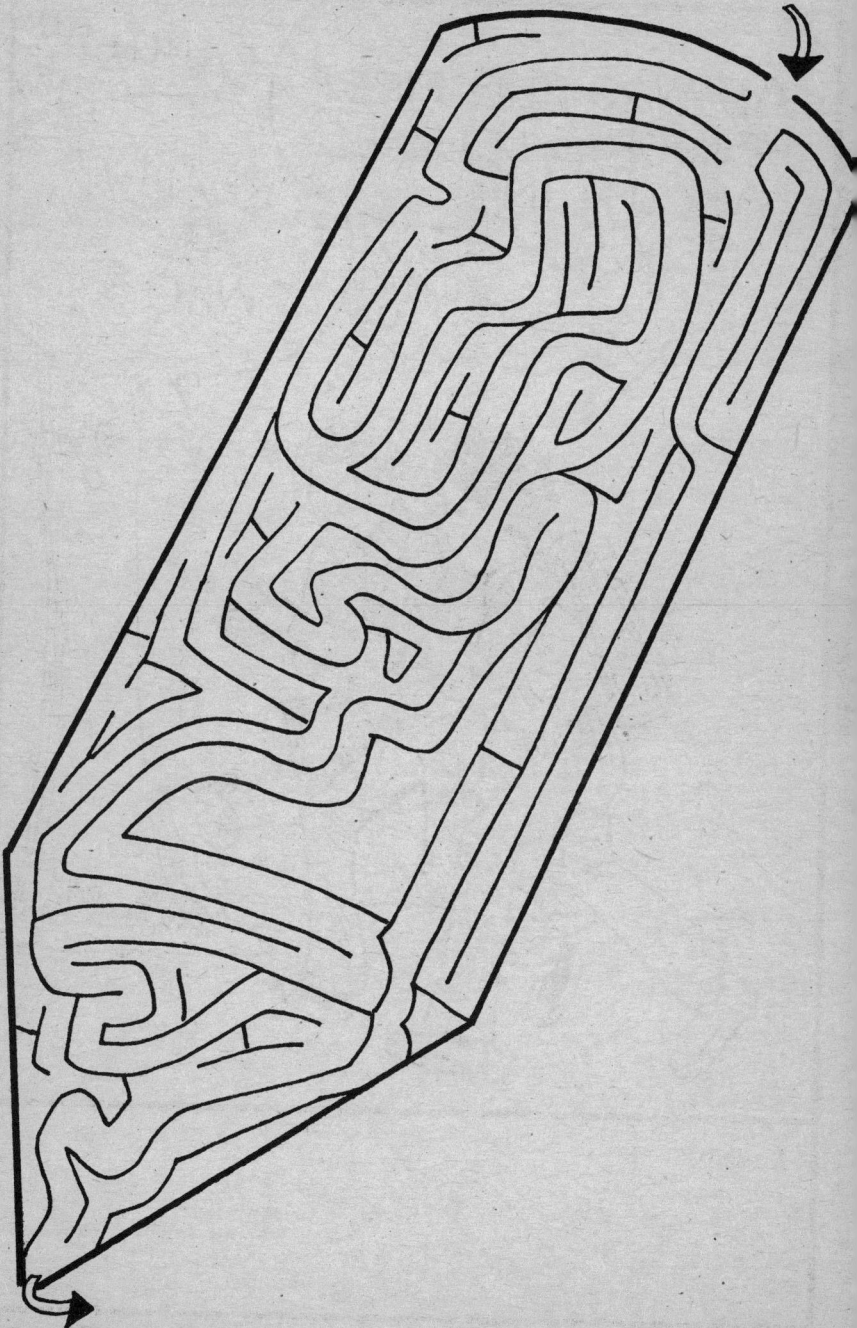

Answer:

SEE ANSWER SECTION

Answer:

How many times does the letter "S" appear in this picture? Circle each one.

TOTAL: _____

SEE ANSWER SECTION

It's recess time! You can reach the ball by following the even numbered path.

To complete the sentence below, circle every **THIRD LETTER** in this puzzle. Then place the circled letters, as they appear, in the spaces below.

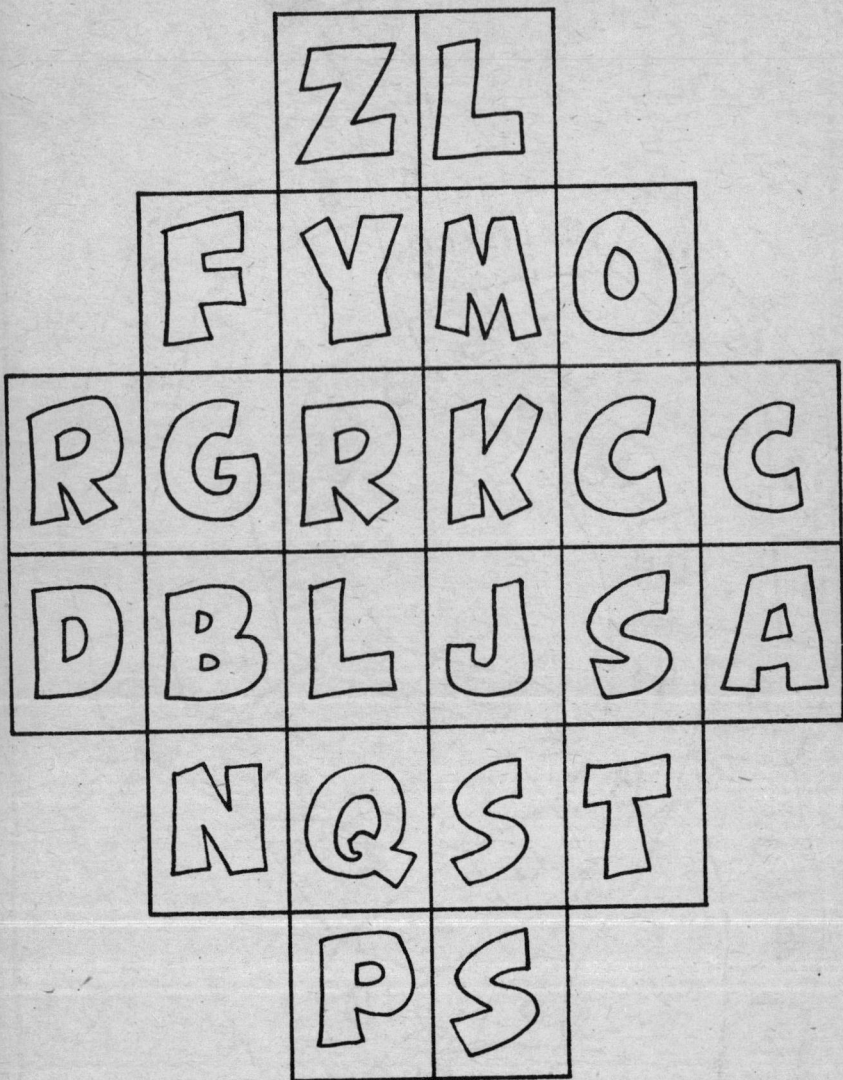

Z L

F Y M O

R G R K C C

D B L J S A

N Q S T

P S

DON'T BE LATE _ _ _ _ _ _ _ _ !

SEE ANSWER SECTION

To reveal the hidden word,
fill in the areas that have a dot •

How many times does the word **TEACH** appear in this puzzle? Circle each one.

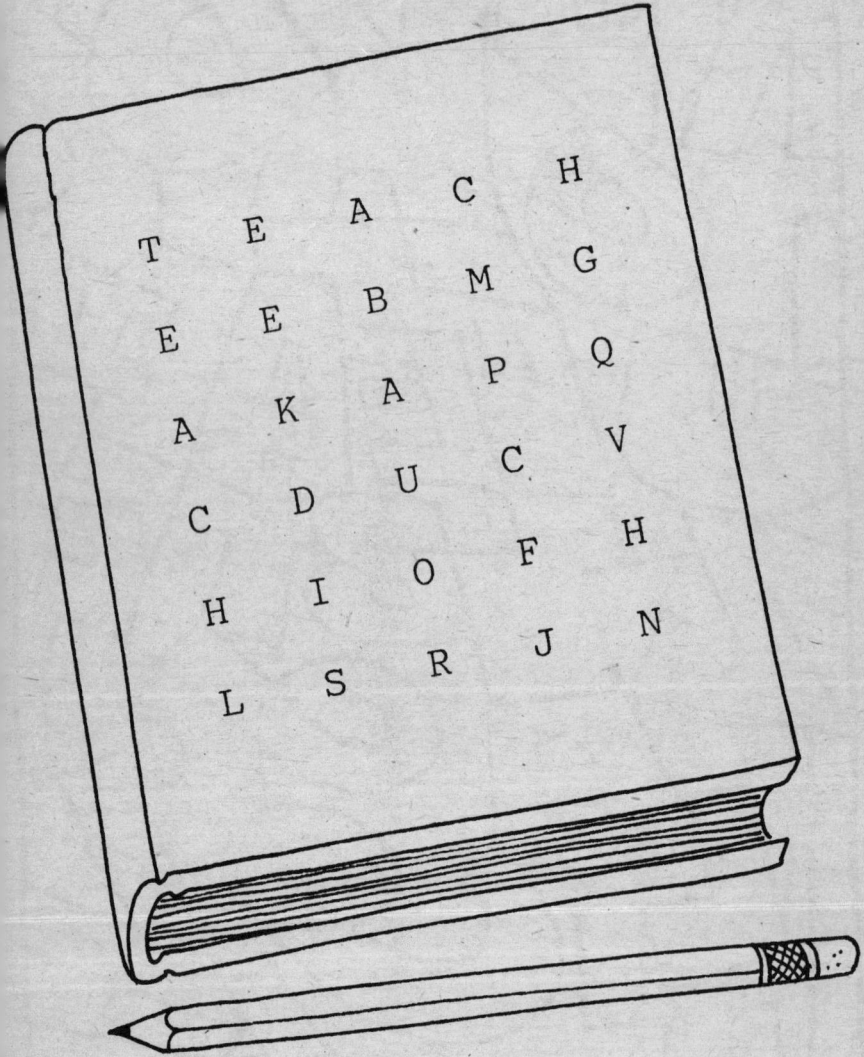

```
    T   E   A   C   H
              B   M   G
  E   E
          A   P   Q
  A   K
      D   U   C   V
  C
          O   F   H
  H   I
      S   R   J   N
  L
```

TOTAL: ____

SEE ANSWER SECTION

Can you find the following hidden objects in this picture?

CAP   STAR   COMB   FEATHER

KITE   SCISSORS   SHOVEL   FORK

SEE ANSWER SECTION

Use this special chart to decode
the message.

A= 7	N= 24
B= 13	O= 12
C= 20	P= 9
D= 3	Q= 17
E= 16	R= 6
F= 2	S= 21
G= 8	T= 15
H= 5	U= 1
I= 10	V= 25
J= 26	W= 4
K= 19	X= 11
L= 23	Y= 22
M= 14	Z= 18

$\overline{10}\ \overline{15}\ '\ \overline{21}$

$\overline{2}\ \overline{1}\ \overline{24}\qquad \overline{15}\ \overline{12}$

$\overline{21}\ \overline{15}\ \overline{1}\ \overline{3}\ \overline{22}$

$\overline{4}\ \overline{10}\ \overline{15}\ \overline{5}$

$\overline{2}\ \overline{6}\ \overline{10}\ \overline{16}\ \overline{24}\ \overline{3}\ \overline{21}\ !$

SEE ANSWER SECTION

Find and circle the two stacks of books that are exactly the same.

Let's go to the cafeteria!
Can you unscramble these words
having to do with lunch?

I M K L   _ _ _ _

U F R T I   _ _ _ _ _

A E T M   _ _ _ _

O K C O I E   _ _ _ _ _ _

K N I R D   _ _ _ _ _

E S T A T   _ _ _ _ _

52

SEE ANSWER SECTION

ANSWER SECTION

page 3

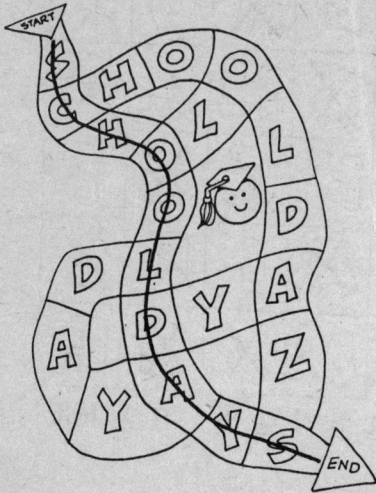

page 4

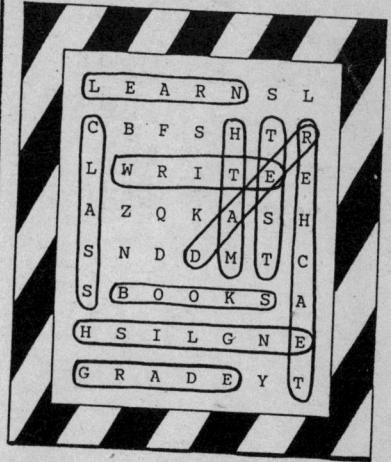

page 5

page 6

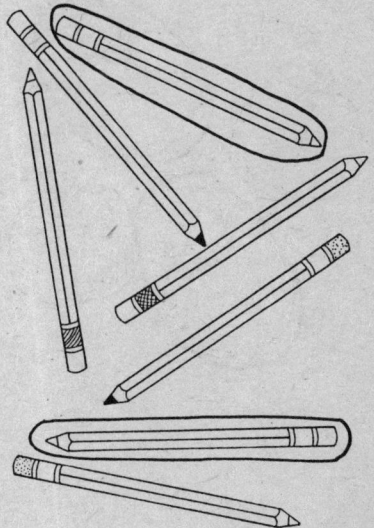

OPPOSITE OF UP. Ⓓ(O)W N
                6

3 PLUS 1 EQUALS **4** . ⒻO U R
                      1

THE MONTH AFTER MAY. J U Ⓝ E
                          5

NOT SMALL. B Ⓘ Ⓖ
              3

YOU HEAR WITH THESE. Ⓔ A Ⓡ S
                     4   2

YOUR TEACHER IS YOUR F R I E N D
                     ‾ ‾ ‾ ‾ ‾ ‾
                     1 2 3 4 5 6

L U N C H   T I M E !
‾ ‾ ‾ ‾ ‾   ‾ ‾ ‾ ‾

THE PRINCIPAL

page 11

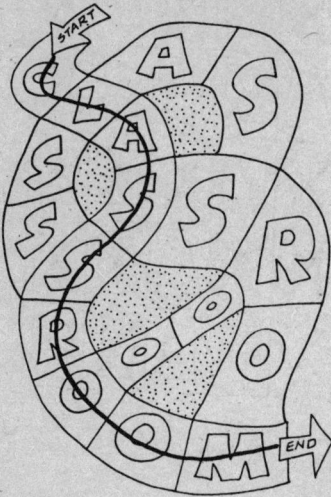

page 12

page 13

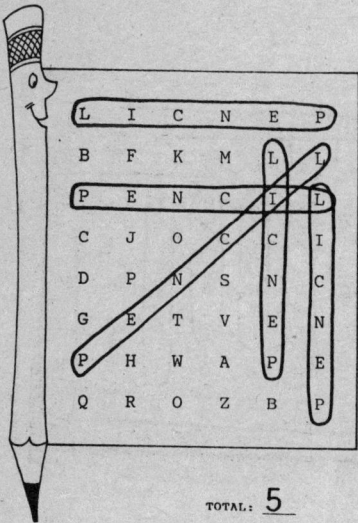

TOTAL: **5**

page 14

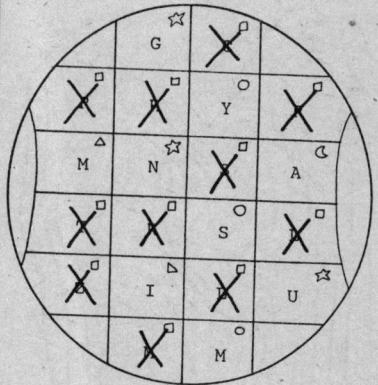

THE G Y M N A S I U M !

page 15

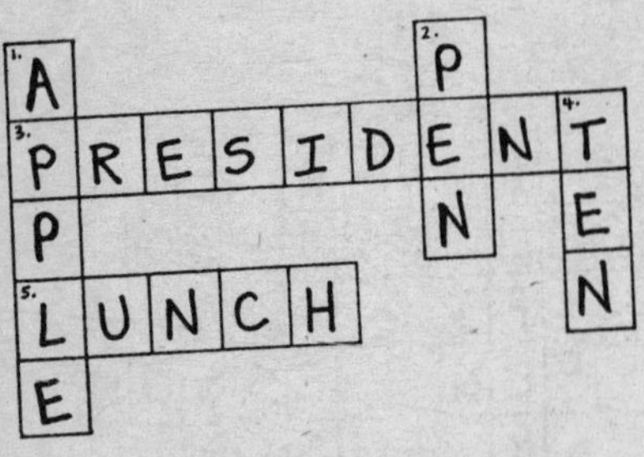

A P P L E (vertical)
P R E S I D E N T
P E N (vertical)
L U N C H
T E N (vertical)

page 16

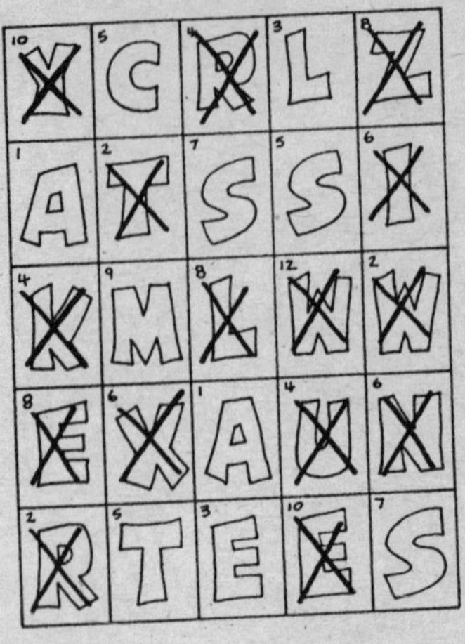

C L A S S M A T E S

page 17

GO

THE LIBRARY
THE PLAYGROUND
THE GYMNASIUM

page 18

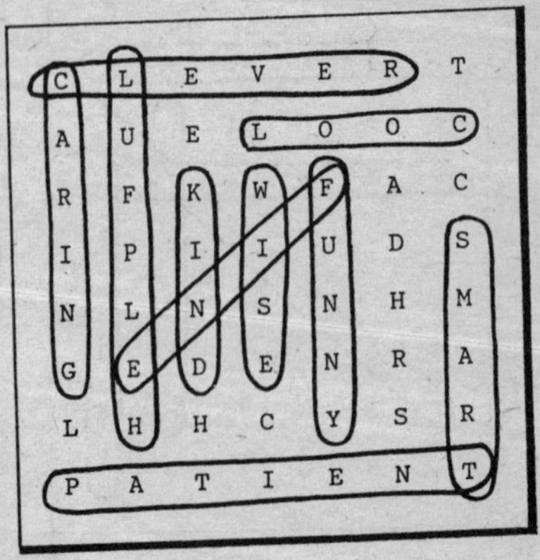

56

page 19

page 20

page 21

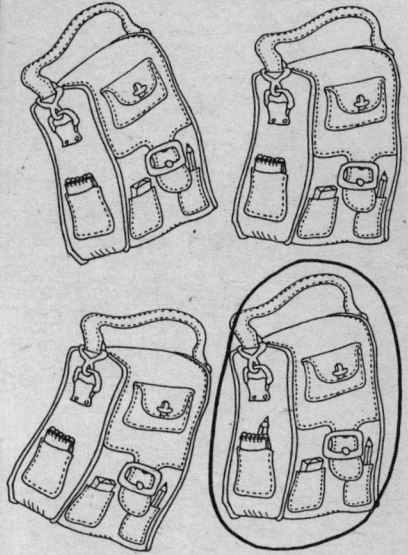

O B K O	**BOOK**
R D E A	**READ**
S L A C S	**CLASS**
U B S	**BUS**
Y L A P	**PLAY**
N R A E L	**LEARN**

page 22

HOMEWORK

TOTAL: **10**

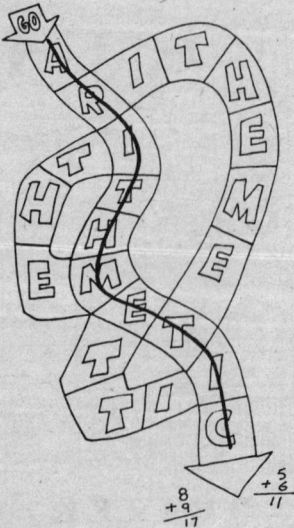

$$\begin{array}{r}8\\+9\\\hline 17\end{array}\qquad\begin{array}{r}5\\+6\\\hline 11\end{array}$$

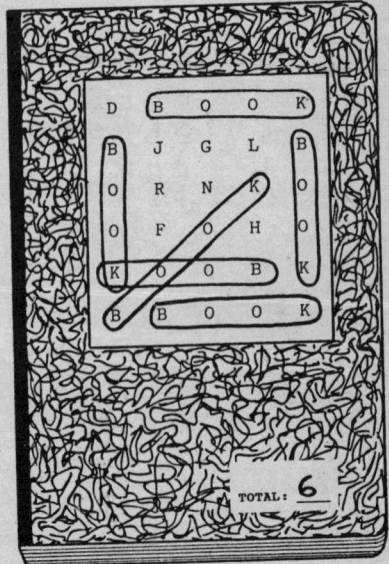

TOTAL: **6**

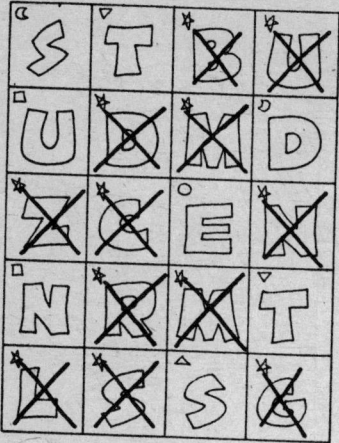

BE KIND TO YOUR FELLOW

<u>S</u> <u>T</u> <u>U</u> <u>D</u> <u>E</u> <u>N</u> <u>T</u> <u>S</u> !

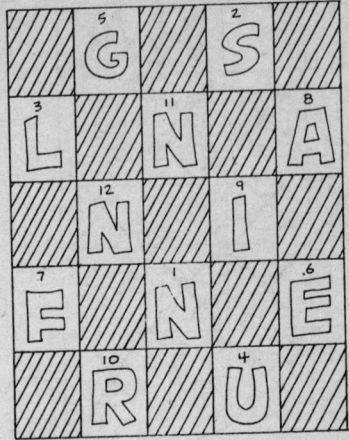

L E A R N I N G   I S
3 6 8 10 1 9 11 5   9 2

F U N !
7 4 12

DAY   N I G H T
         6   2

HAPPY   S A D
         8   4

NORTH   S O U T H
         1   3

FALSE   T R U E
         7   5

S T U D E N T S
1 2 3 4 5 6 7 8

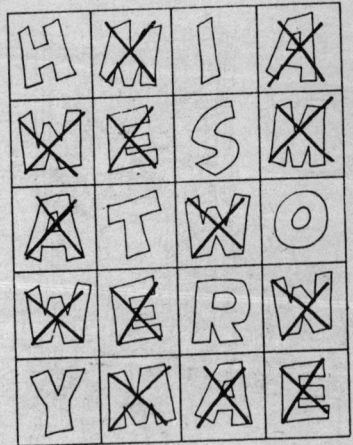

H I S T O R Y

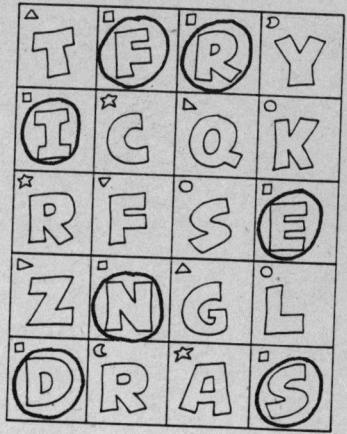

SCHOOL IS A GREAT PLACE TO MAKE

NEW F R I E N D S !

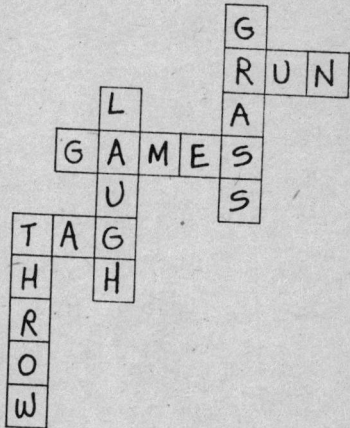

page 39

TOTAL: **10**

page 41

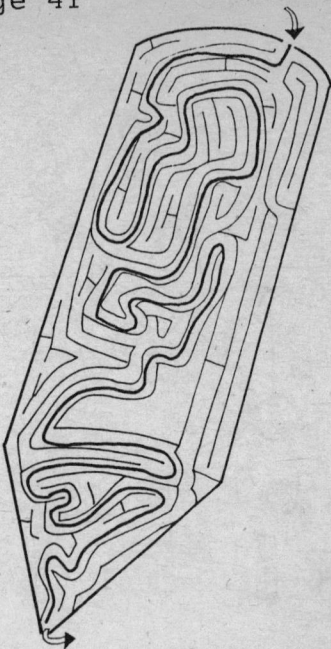

page 42

AL WAS THE FIRST PERSON I LEARNED ABOUT IN SCHOOL!

REALLY! ...AL WHO?

Answer:
AL PHABET!

page 43

WHERE, IN SCHOOL, CAN YOU ALWAYS FIND ICE CREAM?

Answer:
IN THE DICTIONARY!

page 44

TOTAL: **10**

62

page 45

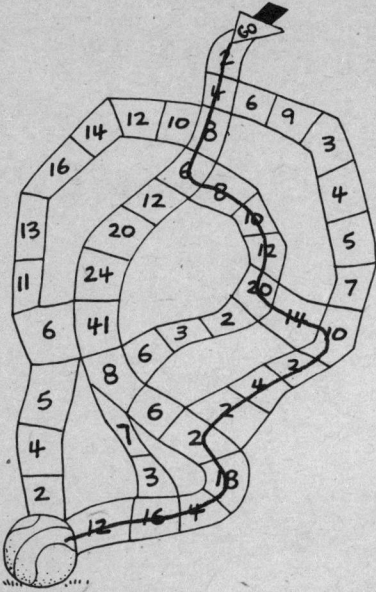

page 46

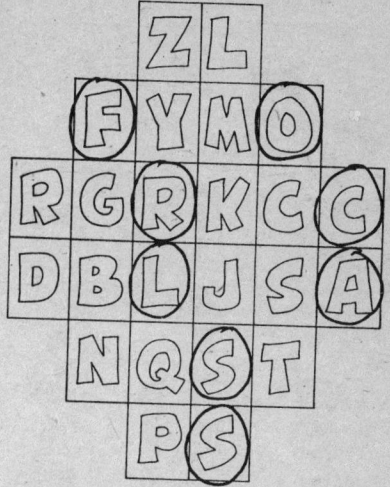

DON'T BE LATE **FOR CLASS**!

page 47

page 48

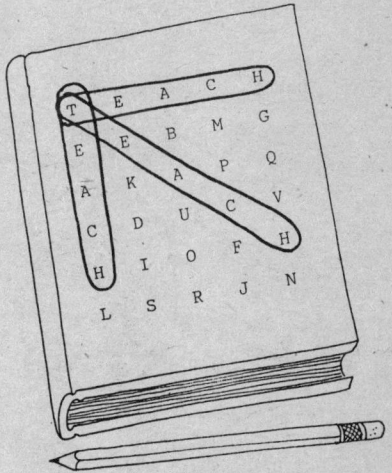

TOTAL: 3

page 49

page 50

A= 7	N= 24
B= 13	O= 12
C= 20	P= 9
D= 3	Q= 17
E= 16	R= 6
F= 2	S= 21
G= 8	T= 15
H= 5	U= 1
I= 10	V= 25
J= 26	W= 4
K= 19	X= 11
L= 23	Y= 22
M= 14	Z= 18

$\underset{10}{I}\ \underset{15}{T}\ .\ \underset{21}{S}$

$\underset{2}{F}\ \underset{1}{U}\ \underset{24}{N}\quad \underset{15}{T}\ \underset{12}{O}.$

$\underset{21}{S}\ \underset{15}{T}\ \underset{1}{U}\ \underset{3}{D}\ \underset{22}{Y}$

$\underset{4}{W}\ \underset{10}{I}\ \underset{15}{T}\ \underset{5}{H}$

$\underset{2}{F}\ \underset{6}{R}\ \underset{10}{I}\ \underset{16}{E}\ \underset{24}{N}\ \underset{3}{D}\ \underset{21}{S}$!

page 51

page 52

I M K L	MILK
U F R T I	FRUIT
A E T M	MEAT
O K C O I E	COOKIE
K N I R D	DRINK
E S T A T	TASTE